# PORTRAIT OF
# THE CAIRNGORMS

GRAHAM UNEY

HALSGROVE

First published in Great Britain in 2009

British Library Cataloguing-in-Publication Data
A CIP record for this title is available from the British Library

ISBN 978 1 84114 882 3

HALSGROVE
Halsgrove House,
Ryelands Industrial Estate,
Bagley Road, Wellington, Somerset TA21 9PZ
Tel: 01823 653777    Fax: 01823 216796
email: sales@halsgrove.com

Part of the Halsgrove group of companies
Information on all Halsgrove titles is available at: www.halsgrove.com

Printed and bound by Grafiche Flaminia, Italy

# INTRODUCTION

I first came to the Cairngorms in the mid 1980s. It was a hot August and I drove through Glenmore Forest from Aviemore ready and eager for the hills. I parked up at Loch Morlich and gazed across the glassy waters to the broadly cut flanks of the Cairngorms to the south. Snow hung in greying ribbons in some of the high gullies and scoops, and had been there since at least the previous winter. I was mesmerised. Snow in August! Later that week I walked across the Cairngorm plateau, a vast area of elevated ground akin to the roughest wilderness tracts of the Arctic tundra, and found an enormous slab of snow resting in the folds around the Feith Buidhe. I sat atop the bouldery ridge that crests the south side of Coire Domhain and watched as a group of walkers went over to explore this slice of old snow. Then, one by one, they disappeared beneath it. This really was quite remarkable, and I just had to go over to explore for myself. What I found both excited and scared the living daylights out of me. A great ice cave, formed where the waters of the Feith Buidhe had carved its way beneath the ice, cut uphill towards the Lochan Buidhe, and far away inside the cave I could hear the voices of the walking group. Pulling on a waterproof jacket I, perhaps a little foolhardy but young enough not to even think about it, walked into the cave and followed it to its end, emerging back onto the sunny hillside a good quarter or a mile or so from where I'd begun. It's true to say that we rarely get winters (or summers) like that in the Cairngorms anymore. Climate change does seem to be effecting the seasons here, and since that first escapade on the plateau I've personally noticed a huge change.

I later went on to train as a mountain guide at Glenmore Lodge, the National Mountain Centre that nestles beneath Cairngorm's Northern Corries, and then ran summer walking and winter mountaineering trips into the Cairngorms for Wilderness Scotland as their Senior Guide. So, I think it's fair to say that I know the Cairngorms pretty well – almost as well as some of the top guides in the business, and certainly better than most non-mountaineering folk!

It's an odd place, the Cairngorms, and I have odd feelings about this range of hills. Most hillwalkers, if asked to name their favourite part of Scotland, would pick the obvious charms of Glencoe, Torridon, Assynt, Knoydart, or perhaps Skye – all rugged mountain ranges or islands rising straight out of the Atlantic, and all very beautiful indeed. You see, over on the west coast of Scotland you get that unique combination of sea and mountain, and it truly is very special indeed. However, whenever I'm asked to name my favourite mountain area, my answer – the Cairngorms – always seems to surprise people. The mountains here are generally rounded, or certainly they appear so from a distance, they are miles away from the sea, and you often have to cover enormous distances just to reach the foot of them. Perhaps that's part of the appeal to me. I love the sense of remoteness you feel in the Cairngorms, and the fact that once you get away from the busy Northern Corries of Cairngorm itself (which is where the main skiing area is) you can walk literally for days and not see another person. I love the wildlife here too, and the vast tracts of ancient Caledonian pine forest that you simply cannot find anywhere else in Scotland to the extent you can in the Cairngorms.

I also love the fact that you really need to know what you're about to go into the Cairngorms. The weather here, on the plateau, is about as bad as it can get. You get winds in excess of 100 miles per hour at times, and huge snow fields that cover the plateau to a depth of thirty or forty feet in places. It's a serious mountain terrain, and to enjoy and survive the Cairngorms you need to respect that. People do die here, even in the summer months – records show that it can (and has) snowed in the Cairngorms on any day of the year.

Generally speaking people think of the Cairngorms as the bit near Aviemore where all the skiing goes on. I like to expand this to take in the other great mountains of the Grampians too, as they all share the same geology (a mass of granite), and have the same character. The Cairngorms National Park, which was established in September 2003, covers much of what I consider to be 'the Cairngorms' although for the purposes of this book I have extended the boundary slightly here and there. I apologise if you disagree with my notion of what is the Cairngorms, but this is a personal collection of images from my experiences in these wonderful mountain ranges.

To the south of the Cairngorms the great glens of the Tilt and Tarf separate the range from the hills of Perthshire, while to the east the range takes in Deeside and Donside, stretching almost to the coast way beyond Mount Keen. To the west, the Drumochter Pass is the border, beyond which the Ben Alder Forest takes over. North of Drumochter we go through Dalwhinnie and into the valley of the River Spey. Here the river separates the Cairngorms to the east from another mountain range, the Monadh Liath. Again, these two hill ranges share very similar characteristics, and as they define the boundaries of Speyside (which is very much the focal point of the Cairngorms) I've also included the eastern part of the Monadh Liath in this book. These two ranges are linked historically too – Monadh Liath means 'Grey Hills', whereas the old name for the Cairngorms was Monadh Ruadh, which means 'Red Hills'. The two ranges were always paired in this way. So, you might ask, what does 'Cairngorm' mean? This is where it gets confusing. Take a look at the Cairngorms from a distance in sunlight and the hills look red (hence Monadh Ruadh), but 'Cairngorm' translates as 'blue stones'. In Victorian times there were a number of Cairngorm hunters living in the region, and these people would go out into the hills in search of the semi-precious blue stones that could be found within the lumps of granite. These 'Cairngorms' gave the mountain range its modern name.

So, the Cairngorms or Am Monadh Ruadh, whichever you prefer, are a mountain range in the middle of the Grampian region of Scotland. There are few human settlements here, and those that do exist – Aviemore, Kingussie, Newtonmore, Braemar, and Ballater are the ones people tend to think of – are scattered generally around the periphery of the hills themselves. This book of photographs depicts the Cairngorm mountains first and foremost. It shows what the Cairngorms are all about, in winter, summer, and the often vague bits of weather in between. I hope that this book will entice you to explore the Cairngorms for yourselves, whether by venturing out into this wild fastness, or by delving deeper into the literary and historical accounts of the Cairngorms that abound. Whichever way you intend to enjoy this magnificent range of mountains – on foot or by armchair – I hope you grow to love the Cairngorms as much as I do, and trust that you will grow to cherish the unique grandeur of these hills.

# LOCATION MAP – Cairngorms

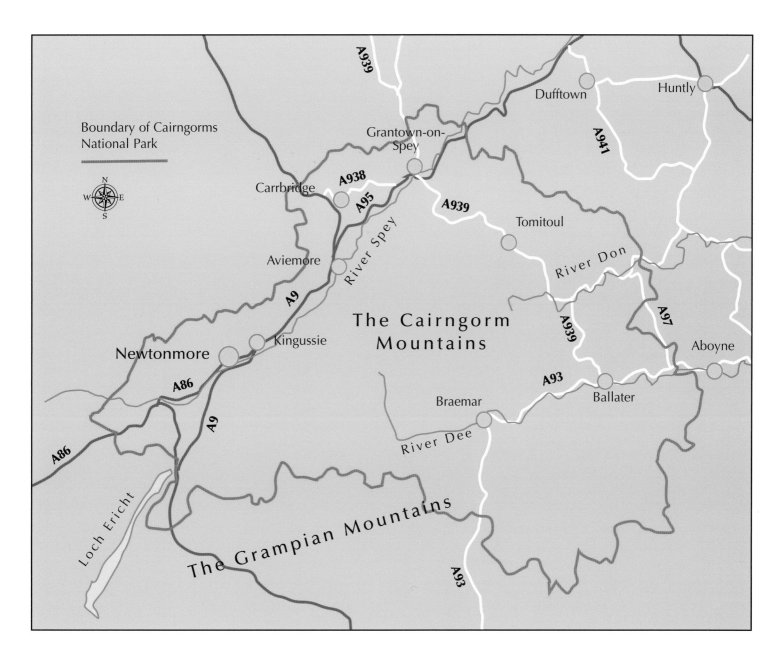

For many people visiting the Cairngorms for the first time, the Cairnwell Pass from Glenshee over to Braemar is the gateway into this magical land. Here snow dusts the rounded slopes of Carn an Tuirc (left) and Carn of Claise (right).

Carn Aosda lies above the Cairnwell Pass, and is a part of the popular Glenshee ski resort.

Winter walkers setting out up Glas Maol from the Glenshee ski centre, with the Carn an Tuirc hills behind.

The huge bowl of Glas Choire holds a crown headwall of late winter snow on Glas Maol.

A walker descending the long ridge of Sron na Gaoithe, the northern spur of Glas Maol, that falls to Seann Spittal Bridge in Glen Clunie.

Crossing the Eidart Bridge at the head of Glen Feshie.

*Below:*
Carn Aosda ski slopes from Glas Maol.

The Geldie Burn cuts across the southern part of the Cairngorm massif, separating the main Cairngorm and Braeriach hills from the peaks of Cairn an Fhidhleir and An Socach.

Approaching the Red House at the confluence of the Geldie Burn and the Bynack Burn.

*Right:*
Across the wild mosses of Inshriach near Kincraig, the Ruthven Barracks guard the marshes. After the defeat at the Battle of Culloden, the remaining Jacobites from Bonnie Prince Charlie's army gathered here to consider how to proceed with the fight against the Hanoverian forces. Whilst at Ruthven they received the order to disperse, and as they fled they burnt down the barracks to prevent the Government forces making use of them.

The beautiful birch and alder woods of the Tromie Glen near Kingussie.

The River Tromie from Tromie Bridge.

A dipper on the River Tromie.

Quartz intrusions
into the bedrock of
Glen Tromie,
making patterns
across the
greyness.

The old farmstead at Baileguish, alongside the Allt Fhearnasdail, one of the many tributaries of the River Feshie.

The view across Glen Feshie towards Sgor Gaoith and Carn Ban Mor from the banks of the Allt Fhearnasdail.

*Right:*
Geal-charn, an outlier of Sgor Gaoith towers above the rocky little peak of Creag Ghuithsachan.

One of the mightiest cirques in the Cairngorms, Coire Garbhlach from Glen Feshie.

Glen Feshie holds important remnants of the ancient Caledonian pine forest, which although being composed chiefly of Scots pine, *Pinus sylvestris*, are also studded with many other wonderful species. Here, a birch tree in its autumn colours stands out vividly against the dark green needles of the pines.

The view up towards the head of Glen Feshie from the bridge at Carnachuin.

Caledonian pine forest cloaks the slopes of Mullach Clach a' Bhlair above Ruigh-aiteachain.

*Above:*
Approaching the bothy at Ruigh-aiteachain, an open shelter that is popular with walkers cutting through the glen from Speyside to Braemar.

*Right:*
The bothy at Ruigh-aiteachain is maintained by the Mountain Bothy Association, and acts as a crucial shelter for walkers.

Walkers rounding the south-west ridge of Mullach Clach a' Bhlair, beneath the crags of Creag na Gaibhre, with the River Feshie rushing through the glen below.

A wild camp high in Glen Feshie.

In the winter the Cairngorms change character completely. Arctic winds sweep across the main Cairngorm plateau, and the corries fill with deep windslab snow. Here in Glen Feshie the wind whistles through the trees.

Walkers carefully approaching the summit of Sgor Gaoith above Glen Feshie. The name, 'Sgor Gaoith' is Gaelic for 'Pointed Peak of the Winds' – very apt!

At the end of a long winter's day a group of walkers descend into Glen Feshie off the Druim nam Bo of Mullach Clach a' Bhlair.

*Left:*
A roe deer fawn or 'kid' in Glen Feshie in the summer.

*Right:*
Kingussie on Speyside, with the rolling hills of the Monadh Liath behind.

A young stonechat fledgling in the Spey Valley.

Right:
A view across the Spey Valley from the foot of Glen Feshie.

*Above:*
A couple of walkers rest on Creag Ghleannain, enjoying the views over Loch Alvie and into the western fringes of the Cairngorms.

*Left:*
To the west of the River Spey, the Monadh Liath rise above Aviemore. Here on Creag Ghleannain above Lynwilg, a cairn marks the best viewpoint.

Mountain hares are common
through the Cairngorm region,
but on Geall-charn Mor,
the mountain above Creag
Ghleannain, there seem to
be hundreds of them running
about the heathery slopes.

Over the 'back' of the Monadh
Liath, beneath Carn an
Fhreiceadain, there lies a
hidden bothy by the headwaters
of the River Dulnain.

The River Dulnain in the Monadh Liath.

High up in the valley of the River Dulnain, where the waters begin their mad rush north-eastwards to eventually join the Spey near Dulnain Bridge.

Red grouse on a warm summer's day in the Monadh Liath.

Back in the main Cairngorm massif, mighty Braeriach's Coire Bhrochain
forms a perfect bowl beneath the summit crags.

*Right:*

In the main Cairngorm massif there are two distinct ranges of mountains. The Cairngorm plateau lies to the east of a huge cleft known as the Lairig Ghru, while to the west of this the Braeriach group forms the second distinct range. Here, Cairn Toul (centre) and Sgor an Lochain Uaine (right) rise above the Lairig Ghru.

*Above:*
The huge valley of the Lairig Ghru slices the Cairngorms in half.

*Left:*
The highest peak of the Cairngorms is Ben Macdui, and this lies immediately east of the Lairig Ghru. Here, the view is of Carn a' Mhaim, from the summit of Ben Macdui.

Evening over the Lairig Ghru from the top of the March Burn.

The March Burn starts high on the flanks of Ben Macdui and tumbles into the Lairig Ghru. The view westwards at sunset over the Lairig Ghru and the Sron na Lairig ridge of Braeriach is spectacular from the top of the March Burn. The mountain in the middle distance with an obvious cleft is Creag Meagaidh.

A young golden eagle soars
through the Lairig Ghru.

Looking through the Lairig Ghru in winter from Creag an Leth-choin (Lurcher's
Crag). The small hill to the right of the glen is the Devil's Point (Bod an Deamhain).

A view of the Lairig Ghru from the Rothiemurchus Forest near Aviemore.

The spectacular slopes of the Lairig Ghru from Whitewell near Aviemore.

Lurcher's Crag with the Lairig Ghru to its right from Whitewell.

Walkers on the summit of Creag an Leth-choin, or Lurcher's Crag.

Exploring the plateau at Ben Macdui's summit, enjoying the views over to Cairn Toul across the Lairig Ghru.

The Sron na Lairig ridge of Braeriach from Ben Macdui.

A male ptarmigan in its summer plumage. In Britain these high altitude birds can only be found on the highest of Scottish mountains.

The summit cairn and Ordnance Survey triangulation pillar on Ben Macdui. The many cairns that are dotted around the summit slopes of Ben Macdui were built during the Second World War by troops of commandos who trained up here. They built them as shelters from the wild weather, and many of them remain to this day.

Looking northwards from the summit of Ben Macdui, along the main path from Cairn Lochan. At the low point where the path appears to start, the March Burn flows to the left into the Lairig Ghru while the Feith Buidhe flows eastwards, to the right and down into the spectacular trench holding Loch Avon.

The wild, open slopes of the Cairngorm plateau from Ben Macdui. Here, the summit cairn and weather station on the top of Cairngorm look deceptively close.

One of the many wonderful things about the Cairngorms is the wildlife. There is a large herd of semi-wild reindeer that wander around the plateau, and here a small group are feeding in Coire Domhain.

Snow lingers in Coire Domhain well into the late summer, and these reindeer like to feed on the mosses, lichens and Alpine plants that grow in these wet areas.

At the head of the Feith Buidhe, on the high pass between Ben Macdui and Cairn Lochan, lies this small lake, the Lochan Buidhe, widely regarded as being the highest lake in Britain.

*Above:*
Looking across the headwaters of Coire Domhain high on the Cairngorm plateau.

*Right:*
A golden plover in its breeding habitat high on the Cairngorm plateau.

The top third of the massive cliffs at Carn Etchachan. Beyond, across the trench that holds Loch Avon, the granite-tor summit of Beinn Mheadhoin (pronounced 'Ben Vane') rises above the scree-covered flanks.

Loch Avon (pronounced 'Loch A'an') forms a perfect focal point to the ring of high mountains at its head. The southern slopes of Cairngorm and Stag Rocks can be seen on the left, while Beinn Mheadhoin fills the view in the distance. To the right lies Shelterstone Crag with Carn Etchachan thrusting up behind.

A male reindeer in Coire Domhain. Reindeer were reintroduced to the Cairngorms from Scandinavia by Mikel Utsi, a Swedish reindeer herder, in 1952.

Looking south from the top of Stob Coire an t-Sneachda, with Beinn Mheadhoin and the crags of Stachan Dubha to the left, and Derry Cairngorm and Carn Etchachan to the right.

*Above:*
Coire Domhain is widely known among mountaineers as 'Snow-hole City'. There is often a huge bank of snow that forms on the south side of the corrie, facing north, and at any point during the winter there will be dozens of snow holes dug into this drift. They are used by the countless outdoor schools that use the Cairngorms as their winter playground. Even in spring you can still see a line of holes below the mini-cornice at the back of the corrie.

*Right:*
Cloud fills the gulf of Coire Lochain, welling out of the gullies and couloirs.

The ptarmigan goes through a number of moults each year,
turning from rock-grey in colour to pure white to blend into its surroundings.

The view down into Coire an t-Sneachda ('Coire' is a hanging valley or cirque in Gaelic, and it has various spellings, including 'Corrie', 'Choire', and 'Coir'. 't-Sneachda' is often mispronounced. It should be pronounced as 'Trayackt'! Its name translates as 'Snow'. So, Coire an t-Sneachda is the hanging valley of snow – very apt!

The twin lochans (small lakes) in the bowl of Coire an t-Sneachda from the top of the Trident Gullies.

Coire an t-Sneachda in summer, with the huge Fiacaill Buttress at the back of the corrie.

*Above:*
Fiacaill Buttress clothed in its winter raiment.

*Left:*
Coire an t-Sneachda in winter. There are various buttresses here, including the Mess of Potage on the far left, Aladdin's Buttress and Fluted Buttress in the centre, and Fiacaill Buttress to the right. All are popular climbing grounds in the winter.

There is a walker's route out of the back of Coire an t-Sneachda. It is known as the Goat Track, and it brings you up onto the plateau between Fluted Buttress and Fiacaill Buttress, giving this stupendous view across to Cairngorm.

Looking down the length of Coire an t-Sneachda as the evening shadows darken and stretch across the boulder fields, from the top of Mess of Potage. The view extends to Loch Morlich, down in the Glenmore Forest.

Stob Coire an t-Sneachda in spring, from the head of Coire Raibert.

The view the other way, from Stob Coire an t-Sneachda to the large cairn at the top of the Fiacaill a' Choire Chais. Coire Raibert runs down to Loch Avon, far below (and out of view) to the right.

A red deer stag in Coire Raibert.

Beinn Mheadhoin from Coire Raibert.

Winter climbers topping out of the various gullies on Stob Coire an t-Sneachda as the sun dips below the hills to the west. The broad gully to the right of the picture is Aladdin's Couloir, a very popular easy winter climb.

Derry Cairngorm's distinctive outline, from the slopes of Cairngorm.

A mountaineer surveys the view from
the summit of Cairngorm.

On Cairngorm's summit is a big cairn, and an automated weather station.

The Cairngorms are a good place to see the tiny snow bunting. This one is perched on a snow fence in the skiing area, no doubt waiting for a few crumbs from the passing skiers.

Walkers descending from the summit of Cairngorm to the Ptarmigan Restaurant, all part of the huge skiing area developed by the company known as 'Cairngorm Mountain'.

Fiacaill a' Choire Chais, with the car park and skiing development in Coire Cas to the right, and Loch Morlich far below.

The 'new' path down the flanks of Fiacaill a' Choire Chais. When the Cairngorm Mountain Company was granted permission to build a funicular almost to the summit of Cairngorm, they laid lots of paved routes into these Northern Corries to alleviate the pressure from the increase in visitor numbers. The whole Cairngorms area is unique in Britain, and is classified as 'Sub-Arctic Tundra'. The plants here grow very slowly, due to the high elevation and latitude, and any damage can take thousands of years to repair itself naturally.

*Above:*
The descent to the skiing area and car park in Coire Cas.

*Left:*
Coire Cas. In winter, this is the main skiing area on Cairngorm.

Snow fences, ski tows, tracks, and of course the funicular, all defile the Northern Corries of the Cairngorms. Let's not forget that this magical, unique environment is supposed to be a National Nature Reserve!

The funicular heads up Cairngorm as a group of walkers heads down.

In winter, gale force winds lift up the spindrift and fresh powder snow, hurling it across the slopes of the mountains. This is Cairngorm from Strath Nethy, and it certainly looks like a good day not to be on its wild slopes!

Cairngorm from across the Braes of Abernethy. Even at this distance the huge scar of the funicular can be seen leading up towards the summit.

To the east of Strath Nethy the isolated lump of Bynack More is a superb Munro.

Bynack More in winter. The smaller hill to the right is Bynack Beg.

There is a wonderfully mystical pass leading north from Glenmore towards the Braes of Abernethy. This is the Ryvoan Pass, or the Thieves Pass. Cattle thieves used to drive the stolen animals through here and southwards to the markets of the Central Belt. This view is of Ryvoan from the slopes of Meall a' Bhuachaille.

At the heart of the Ryvoan Pass is the wonderful An Lochan Uaine, or the Green Lake. Here in winter, it is frozen solid.

Splendid remnants of the ancient Caledonian pine forest, the old woodland that once clothed much of the Highlands. These Scots pines, *Pinus sylvestris*, cling to the steep scree slope above An Lochan Uaine in the Pass of Ryvoan.

Wild weather above Ryvoan, as the wind whips snow across the flanks of Creag nan Gall.

Better winter conditions. A group of walkers head up Meall a' Bhuachaille under blue skies.

*Above:*
In summer the Ryvoan Pass is a very different place. The route through the pass is popular with walkers, cyclists, and birdwatchers – the land here is all part of a massive RSPB Reserve. There is a small bothy here too, that is always busy.

*Right:*
Meall a' Bhuachaille towards the Ryvoan Bothy.

*Left:*
Red grouse abound in the Braes of Abernethy.

*Right:*
The view over Loch Morlich and Glenmore Forest from the summit of Meall a' Bhuachaille.

*Left:*
A huge summit cairn adorns the highest point of Meall a' Bhuachaille. The hill's name translates as the 'Bare Hill of the Shepherd'.

The Braes of Abernethy.

*Left:* The view to the north-east from the summit of Meall a' Bhuachaille, towards the distant Hills of Cromdale.

The path that leads up Bynack More (on the far right), across the Braes of Abernethy.

The Braes of Abernethy are prime nesting ground for a number of bird species. Red and black grouse nest on the moors, along with stonechat, meadow pipit, and red-throated divers on the lochs, while the pine forests hold nationally important numbers of capercaillie, crossbill and crested tit.

The lovely, tranquil waters of Loch Mallachie, deep in the heart of the Abernethy Forest.

Perfect reflection in Loch Mallachie.

Loch Mallachie lies at the centre of the RSPB's land in Abernethy Forest. Wood sandpipers, goldeneye, crested tits, capercaillie, and Scottish crossbill all nest here.

Loch Mallachie is a truly magical place, full of drama, stark outlines, and wide vistas.

The old bridge at Carrbridge. This old packhorse bridge is the oldest in the Highlands, and was erected in 1717 by Brigadier-General Sir Alexander Grant of Grant. It took six months to build, and cost the estate £100.

The wooden bridge at Broomhill spans the River Spey.

Fly fishing for sea trout on the River Spey at Broomhill.

A roe deer doe in the summer meadows of the Spey Valley near Broomhill.

The distinctive cone of Carn Eilrig from the Rothiemurchus Forest.

Cairngorm from near Dorback Lodge, across the Braes of Abernethy. Even in summer the last of the winter snows still cling to the mountainsides in large pockets.

The Cairngorms from the Braes of Abernethy.

*Right:*
Let's not forget whisky! Speyside is one of the most important regions for whisky distilling in Scotland. There are many great single malts from which to choose, and many of the distilleries have visitor centres and tours for the visitor to enjoy. This is 'The Glenlivet', one of the more popular brands, and the only Scottish distillery to define itself by adding 'The' to its name!

*Left:*
To the north of the Braes of Abernethy the low rolling curves of the Hills of Cromdale rise from the moor.

*Right:*
On the Cromdale Hills a curlew has found a good nesting site among the heather and rough moorland grasses.

In the east of the Cairngorms, the lesser known hills roll down to the Rivers Dee and Don. On the south side of the Lecht, the high pass between Tomintoul and Ballater, Corgarff Castle stands aloof above the braes. The castle was probably built in the 1550s by John Forbes of Towie, and was of great importance as it guarded the cross country route between Deeside and Speyside.

Winter returns to the Cairngorms, and wild storms sweep across the eastern hills above Cock Bridge.

The view up Glen Gairn towards Brown Cow Hill.

Between Gairnshiel Lodge and Crathie, by the side of the B976, you can often spot mountain hares. This one has turned into its winter pelage of grey-white.

Vast moorlands studded with great architectural pines rise in folds to the snow-shrouded mountains above Glen Quoich.

Scattered pines in Glen Quoich. This is typical of how the ancient forests would have looked, rather than being dense.

Quoich Water and Beinn a' Bhuird. These remote mountains of the eastern Cairngorms are little visited, particularly in winter.

Pine and birch grow happily together, allowing plenty of light through to the undercover. Beinn a' Bhuird lies dusted in snow behind.

Heading along the landrover track towards distant Beinn a' Bhuird.

*Above:*
The speckled hill, Beinn Bhreac from high in Glen Quoich.

*Left:*
A magnificent twisted pine in Glen Quoich.

Granite frosted into position in Glen Quoich.

Looking up towards the massive plateau of Beinn a' Bhuird, the view from An Diollaid.

Once on the Beinn a' Bhuird plateau, the whole atmosphere changes as you feel the grips of winter tearing across the tundra.

Massive cornices, waves of snow, guard the rim of Coire nan Clach on Beinn a' Bhuird's summit slopes. The distant tors of Leabaidh an Daimh Bhuidhe and the Ben Avon massif dominate the views to the north-east.

To the south of Braemar and the River Dee the mountains rise again to the hills of the White Mounth and Lochnagar. Here, at Loch Callater, the waters are held still by the grip of winter.

The old stables at Lochcallater Lodge are now used as a bothy, and give a fine refuge from the weather for mountaineers heading onto the surrounding Munros.

In the White Mounth in winter the views come and go as the clouds are torn apart by the wind.

Tackling the long walk between Carn an t-Sagairt Mor and Lochnagar.

Camping high in the mountains in the Cairngorms is a challenge at any time of year, but in the winter months it requires a lot of planning, training, and experience. This high camp is just below the final summit dome of Carn an t-Sagairt Mor in the White Mounth.

The magnificence of The Stuic above Coire Loch nan Eun.

The highest point of Lochnagar is the peak at the northern end of the long summit ridge. The summit is known as Cac Carn Beag, and it is marked by an Ordnance Survey triangulation pillar overlooking the wild north-east corrie.

The way into the hills from the south-east – a footpath sign at the point where Glen Mark and Glen Lee merge to form the main valley, Glen Esk.

A rugged red deer stag in Glen Mark.

The Queen's Well in Glen Mark – a spot favoured by Queen Victoria.

Glen Mark is wonderfully wild in its upper reaches. Craig of Doune splits the valley and the Water of Mark squeezes through a gorge to its south.

The Water of Mark plunges over a number of impressive waterfalls. Here at White's Pool the river passes over bedrock at the base of Craig of Doune.

A male wheatear high in Glen Mark.

Looking up Glen Lee from Westbank above Glen Esk.

Charr Bothy in Glen Dye, way out east of the National Park, but still very Cairngorm in character.

Dropping down to Tarfside in Eskdale.

At the head of Glen Dye, where the main river splits. The Water of Dye flows down to here from the west, while the Burn of Badymicks comes in from the north-west. Both branches drain Mount Battock, which fills the horizon to the west.

Grouse are all part of the economy in the Cairngorms. To maintain a healthy grouse moor you need to provide shelter, in the form of old heather stems, as well as plenty of food for the grouse. Red grouse eat mainly fresh heather shoots, so large patches of heather are burnt every year to promote new growth.

The warty tor of granite on the summit of Clachnaben from the Drumtochty Forest across Glen Dye.

A scattering of snow on Clachnaben from the Old Military Road at Spittal Cottage.